STUART DAVIS

The Great American Artists Series

ALBERT P. RYDER *by Lloyd Goodrich*

THOMAS EAKINS *by Fairfield Porter*

WINSLOW HOMER *by Lloyd Goodrich*

WILLEM de KOONING *by Thomas B. Hess*

STUART DAVIS *by E. C. Goossen*

JACKSON POLLOCK *by Frank O'Hara*

IN PREPARATION

JOHN JAMES AUDUBON *by Ruthven Todd*

JOHN MARIN *by Kenneth Sawyer*

BEN SHAHN *by James Thrall Soby*

ARSHILE GORKY *by Harold Rosenberg*

Stuart
DAVIS

by E. C. Goossen

Distributed by Pocket Books, Inc.

GEORGE BRAZILLER, INC.
NEW YORK   1959

LIBRARY OF CONGRESS CATALOG CARD NUMBER: 59–12223

PRINTED IN THE UNITED STATES OF AMERICA
BY R. R. DONNELLEY & SONS COMPANY

CONTENTS

ACKNOWLEDGMENTS

I WISH to take advantage of this opportunity to thank Mrs. Edith Gregor Halpert, of the Downtown Gallery, for her generous assistance and for permitting me to glean from her handsomely kept files much of the information and many of the photographs used in the preparation of this book.

I should also like to thank Mr. John Marin, Jr., Mrs. Halpert's assistant, for his kind co-operation in obtaining photographs from many sources. And thanks are due to Mr. Holger Cahill who talked lengthily with me about his friend, the artist, and the history of the Art Project days.

Finally, of course, I must thank Mr. Davis with whom I had a number of fine hours just talking things over.

E.C.G.

STUART DAVIS

Photograph by Marvin P. Lazarus

Little Giant Still Life. 1950. Oil, 33 x 43″. Virginia Museum

I did not spring into the world fully equipped
to paint the kind of pictures I want to paint.[1]

NEARLY FIFTY YEARS have passed since Stuart Davis, age six-
teen, entered Robert Henri's school and began to devote himself intensively to the problems of painting. Today he stands forth,
a singular figure among the painters of our time, both in the United
States and abroad. The amazing continuity of his painting and
the constancy of his principles through one of the most hectic
and harrowing periods in the history of art have placed him in
a position calling forth an admiration even his bitterest critics
have been unable to deny him. Davis' art, aloof, absolute
and personal, is impossible to submerge into a school with

11

smaller fish. It is an art so resolutely founded in principle that even when an individual painting can be judged unsuccessful it suggests the fineness of the principles behind it. At a moment when vagueness about pictorial structure is being used to support all kinds of rationalizations after the fact, Davis' clean-cut assertions make weaker painters uneasy. The best of the younger artists, however, recognize and respect what he stands for and thus assure the permanence of his position in the chronology of American (now International) painting. The larger public, mesmerized by the violent and episodic careening of modern art and artists, often seems to have forgotten that painting is an art involving composition as well as personality. Astute eyes, however, have never turned away from Davis. They see why and how he has purposefully and patiently worked to create again and again the kind of pictures he wanted to paint, pictures with the kind of pictorial structure which characterizes the best in the greatest painting traditions. And when the younger artists are howling about *commitment,*[2] they need only turn to Davis for an example of the highest order.

Davis' commitment began earlier than most. He was born and bred in a home where it was known that art existed, a fortunate and relatively unusual situation in turn-of-the-century America. His father[3] was art editor of the *Philadelphia Press* and among his employees were the young artists, John Sloan, William Glackens, Everett Shinn and George Luks, half of the group later to be famous as "The Eight."[4] Davis' family moved to the vicinity of New York at about the same time another Philadelphia artist, Robert Henri,[5] came to the big city and opened his famous art school which, as Davis has reported, "was regarded as radical and revolutionary in its methods, and it was."[6] Henri's school in 1910 was, as Hans Hofmann's was to become in the 1940's,[7] the center of art activity in New York and the breeding place for the pictures that dominated the American scene for the next several decades. "All the usual art school routine was repudiated. Individuality of expression was the key-

12

note, and Henri's broad point of view in his criticism was very effective in evoking it. Art was not a matter of rules and techniques, or the search for an absolute ideal of beauty. It was the expression of ideas and emotions about the life of the time . . . Enthusiasm for running around and drawing things in the raw ran high."[8]

This was the moment when America's last cultural battle with Europe was shaping up, a battle which, though some vestigial and petty issues still persist, ended only recently when America realized its old debt to Europe had been paid off by two wars and one self-awakening Depression. The guilty son, having established his separateness, could finally make an affectionate peace with his father. Henri, in sending his students out to draw the American scene in the raw and to rely on their own emotional responses to local subjects rather than on arty academic methods, perhaps had to charge them with an emotional chauvinism so that they could learn to value their own vision. An artist without his own vision, irrespective of nationality, is nothing more than a mechanical clod (what we mean by *academic*), but to release that vision from its artistic repressions is the hardest thing for a teacher to accomplish (assuming he *wants* to). Henri accomplished more than he might have desired in Davis' case, for the latter says, "the emphasis on subject matter, which was implicit in the whole Henri idea, tended to give subject matter, as such, a more important place than it deserves in art."[9] And when he complains that Henri "in repudiating academic rules for picture structure" was unable to establish "new ones suitable to the new purpose"[10] we can see that Davis, for one, was a person who found floundering in a sea of relativities uncomfortable.

The borderline between descriptive and illustrative painting, and art as an autonomous sensate object, was never clarified.[11]

13

In a sense the revolution of "The Eight" (the four from Philadelphia plus Henri, Ernest Lawson, Arthur B. Davies and Maurice Prendergast) was social rather than artistic. Its effect on American art is reminiscent of what occurred in French painting sixty years before with the appearance of the iconoclastic and earthy pictures of Daumier and Courbet and the naturalistic social novels of Emile Zola. But by the very provocation of its subject matter, the Ash Can School, as it was labeled, undoubtedly drew an attention to art in this country unexampled before in our history. Unlike French socialist movements, American liberalism had tended to be sentimental and Whitmanesque. In the first twenty years of this century it grew bitterer, challenging an American democratic pride often hollow at the core. Cartoons in *The Masses*[12] were one thing, but genuine oil paintings of Irish servant girls undressing in tenements intended to be hung in fashionable salons were quite another. Vilification only added to the general interest. And as the erotic elements in the great painting of the past had often made it saleable to people for whom its *art* was impenetrable, the new subject matter (frequently mere dramatized journalism, including a report on the artist's enthusiasm through his slap-dash brushwork) exposed some otherwise blind spectators to things they would have to deal with in the not too distant future.

Davis succumbed to this American-scene realism for a time and never really abandoned the liberalistic attitudes he acquired then. But his idealism had a hierarchy. He was first and foremost an artist, as he proved when he resigned from *The Masses* because an editorial group headed by Max Eastman, Art Young and John Reed insisted that his, Sloan's and the other artists' work should conform more closely to the socialist ideals of the magazine. And he indirectly proved again that politics were at most second in his hierarchy of values when, during the harsh days of the Depression Thirties, though an important office-holding member of the Artists Congress[13] and deeply involved in the

14

Davits. 1932. Brush and ink, 20¾ x 28½″. Fogg Art Museum, Harvard University

leftist politics of the day, his style remained unpopularly and un-
politically abstract, as far from propagandistic social realism as
any art could be.

The International Exhibition of Modern Art, now known as
the Armory Show,[14] was held in 1913, and Davis exhibited five
watercolors in the American section. It was this show which exposed the young artist to the revolutionary painting going on in
Europe at the time. There he saw for the first time examples of
Cubism and the Fauve work of Matisse, as well as the older
painting of the late nineteenth century by Gauguin and van
Gogh. What affected him most in these painters were the "broad

15

generalizations of form and the non-imitative use of color . . . practices within my own experience . . ." and he ". . . also sensed an objective order in these works which I felt was lacking in my own."[15] The Cubist painting in the show perhaps did not affect him so much then, though eventually some of its aesthetics, in combination with the brilliant non-local color of the Fauves,[16] were to form the basis from which he would arrive at his own inimitable style.

In a way Davis had to fill in the gaps left by American painting before he could achieve his desire "to become a 'modern' artist." Assisted to a more complete understanding of the new French art by Charles Demuth,[17] whom he met that year in Provincetown, he began first by catching up with van Gogh. In several pictures painted from 1916 to 1919 (plates 2–6, 17) it is apparent he was already overtaking the Dutch master, while not yet able to release himself from van Gogh's seductive manner. In *Rockport Beach* (plate 17), having taken a high viewpoint, Davis proceeds to pull the distant portions of the observed landscape, if not quite up to the surface of the canvas, at least forward enough to destroy the usual gradient toward the horizon. In *Landscape* (plate 3, which is probably one of the first "all-over" paintings by an American) the thickly brushed and textured paint spreads the unfocused scene with the same intensity from edge to edge. (Davis, obviously, was already involved with twentieth-century painting, definable, in part, as the general acceptance of the flat reality of the canvas surface.) The hedgerows and the harshly treated contours of sea, woods and shore in *Rockport Beach* tend toward the same flattening effect; the bold crudity in the drawing of the beach is prophetic of the raw, American shapes to appear later in the work of Marsden Hartley, Arshile Gorky[18] and in many recent Abstract-Expressionist pictures.

Davis' experience at Provincetown was similar to van Gogh's when he went to the south of France. "On clear days," Davis says, "the air and water had a brilliance of light greater than I had ever seen, and while this tended to destroy local color it stimulated the desire to invent high intensity color-intervals."[19] Thus he became thoroughly aware that, as the Fauves had bluntly stated in their pictures, color, as far as art was concerned, could be completely abstracted from the objects it was associated with in nature. Color was a thing to be used in art, rather than imitated.

The subject matter of painting includes the materials of expression.[20]

In the next few years Davis experimented with the collage technique invented by Braque and Picasso in 1912 and growing in popularity among all the Cubists. He, too, pasted pieces of paper on the surface of his canvases, often varying the procedure by painting imitations of the wall-paper, labels and other objects used by the French Cubists. By imitating rather than actually using the labels of such things as cigarette packages, etc., Davis destroyed, in one sense, the essence of collage, but freed himself from the limitations of the size of the objects. Though his own method may have been a misunderstanding of what the others were after, it nevertheless gave him an insight into where subject matter could be found and how it could be transposed and composed into a picture. With these "imitated" collages of 1921 (plate 7) he first introduces words and letters, elements one day to comprise an important part of his pictorial vocabulary (an interest traceable perhaps to his father's sign-painter and news-paper career). At the same time he learned how to dispose upon the canvas selected color-shapes in such a manner as not to violate the surface, though it would be many years before he would apply the principle exclusively. Words and letters, moreover, belong to the world of surfaces and their appearance unattached to anything represented volumetrically makes doubly sure (psy-

17

chologically and through the conventions of our visual experience) that the plane of the canvas will be unequivocally confirmed. In *Cigarette Papers* (plate 8) one can easily see how the use of the words identifies the surface precisely as the place where the picture occurs. The two volumetric representations, the printed ribbon in the upper right and the cord along the bottom extend *outward* toward us in one of the few types of illusion permitted in Cubist and post-Cubist painting—permitted because it both denies that a picture is just a flat decorative poster and yet fits the refusal of our age to accept any illusion other than the one which nakedly confesses itself.

Davis went to Havana in 1918 and to New Mexico in 1923, but in neither place did he feel as much at home as he did in New York and Gloucester, the latter having replaced Provincetown as his summer retreat. He gave up painting directly from nature, bringing his pen sketches back to the studio where he began to synchronize various landscapes into one picture. Such a synthesis of scenes had already been pre-visioned in his *Multiple Views* (plate 4), one of those bastard composites which breaks all rules of pictorial and visual logic and fails to achieve even a minimal solution. In this case, the desired end was simultaneity. (During the 1930's this illegitimately conceived manner of kaleidoscoping history spread over the walls of our post-offices, shedding aesthetic darkness over all who came to mail a letter.)[21] The historical value of Davis' *Multiple Views,* however, lies in the way it illuminates one aspect of the principled completeness Davis was seeking. How could one collapse time and space into "a single focus," one simultaneous vision? Again Cubist practise could assist, for in its fragmentation of observed volumetric forms, re-presented as skins and essences pressed flat upon the canvas, many views of a subject were recorded as one. Thus the element of time could be captured within a picture. The Futurists attempted to make this explicit by trying to record abstract essences of real motion; the Cubists left it implicit—as the artist's vision instead of the subject's condition.

18

Composition No. 4. 1934. Ink drawing, 21¼ x 29¾". The Museum of Modern Art, gift of Mrs. John D. Rockefeller, Jr.

Synchronizing his landscapes into "a single focus," however, brought new problems; in order to achieve the unity lacking in *Multiple Views* it was necessary "to select and define the spatial limits of these separate drawings." He would have to have "an objective attitude toward positional relations," and "having already achieved this to a degree in relations of color, the two had to be integrated and thought about simultaneously."[22] He had begun to think in terms of what he later called "color-space."

It no longer made any difference what subject matter he chose, whether landscape or the kind of still-lifes Cézanne had painted in order to analyse form in terms of planes of color. The pictorial organization was now what really mattered to Davis.

In *Apples and Jug* (plate 9) he solved his "spatial limit" in a relatively easy way. By laying the shadows on the apple in

19

the foreground in a flat and geometrical denial of its roundness, he drives it back while allowing the apple in the rear to take on some of its natural volume. In addition, the ground line at the left does not appear on the right, with the result that background is identified with the canvas while some illusion of space is still retained. It is a good but clever picture, playing on obvious visual paradoxes, like so many of Léger's paintings from the same general period. Davis has always included the French painter among his influences, as well as Seurat, whom he cites for his sense of space rather than his color (Davis considers the dotted areas in his own pictures as serving *textural* implications before they are anything else). He had also looked intently at Japanese woodblock prints, especially Hokusai,[23] whose wavy line appears as simulated wood-grain on the front of the *Super Table* (plate 14).

Davis has said of these pictures of 1924–25 that they "were all based on the same idea; a generalization of form in which the subject was conceived as a series of planes and the planes as geometrical shapes—a valid view of the structure of any subject . . . these geometrical planes were arranged in direct relationship to the canvas as a flat surface . . . In paintings like *Super Table,* the major relationships . . . were established, but the minor features were still imitative."[24]

Gradually through this concentration I focused on the logical elements.[25]

Because he was pursuing a logical course, or, as he put it himself "groping towards a structural concept,"[26] accepting the labor and the moral discipline necessary to the creation of an authentic personal aesthetic, Davis' next step is not so surprising. But it does speak of a kind of dogged heroism unfamiliar today and of a determination perhaps only comparable to Cézanne's.

He now had a number of sufficiently clear and co-ordinated concepts as to how one might go about painting a picture. There was nothing left to do but make some pictures by means of them. In 1945 he wrote of his experiences in 1927–28. "One day I set up an eggbeater in my studio and got so interested in it that I nailed it on the table and kept it there to paint. I called the pictures *Eggbeater,* number such and such, because it was from the eggbeater that the pictures took their impulse . . . Their subject is an invented series of planes which was interesting to the artist. They were then drawn in perspective and light and shade in the same way another artist draws the planes of a human head or a landscape. They were a bit on the severe side, but the ideas involved in their construction have continued to serve me . . . I got away from naturalistic forms. I invented these geometrical elements. Gradually through this concentration I focused on the logical elements. They became the foremost interest . . . I felt that a subject had its emotional reality fundamentally through our awareness of . . . planes and their spatial relationships . . . My aim was not to establish a self-sufficient system to take the place of the immediate and the accidental, but to . . . strip a subject down to the real physical source of its stimulus . . . So you may say that everything I have done since has been based on that eggbeater idea. I have just tried to carry the idea into greater particularity without abandoning the general scope which interested me there."[27]

Though according to Davis the *Eggbeaters* were "drawn in perspective and light and shade" one need only study *Eggbeater No. 3* (plate 16) to see, even in black and white, that this is perspective with a difference. Everywhere what is suggested as setting up directional depth *inward* is frustrated by the interruption of the plane or line stopping the eye's journey, turning it along a new path, only to be turned shortly again. Curves emanating from points tangent to the edge of another plane slide the eye

21

around, leading it always back to the *recognition* of the flat rectangle of the canvas. And though there is a suggestion of "light and shade," just where it comes from is impossible to determine. (Cézanne had destroyed the sense of light issuing from one source by purposely painting shadows on different sides of different buildings in many of his pictures. He still needed light in order to create form, but he did not want to create a deep space and thus damage the reality and the unity of the canvas surface.) Part of what one might call the calculated ambiguity of form and space in Davis' later pictures derives from the same sort of anti-perspective perspective he began to employ in the *Eggbeaters.* It is at this time that he conceived and began to render pictorially the underlying philosophy of his art, the principle of ambiguous relations—all elements shall appear in unity and simultaneously, and each element, to take only the compositional ones, shall serve more than one purpose. *Color,* for example, shall also be *space.* ("Color must be thought of as texture which automatically allows one to visualize it in terms of space.") *Line* shall also be *direction; plane* also *color* and *form;* and *form* itself, which can only exist in space, and *space,* which can only be meaningful through form, shall in every possible instance stand for each other. The ideal is classical in that it aims for a unity stemming from the sum of parts. The rhythmical relations between these parts, however, is modern, deriving from the facts of modern life, the speed with which we travel—"An artist who has traveled on a steam train, driven an automobile, or flown in an airplane doesn't feel the same way about form and space as one who has not."[28]

Scientific knowledge and its effect upon everything around us has changed all our notions about the way the world is put together. The structure of nature is no longer a matter of appearances but susceptible to our surgical logic probing through its inner organization.

22

*I had looked at my eggbeater so long that I
finally had no interest in it.*[29]

The sale of several pictures in 1928 gave Davis the opportunity to go to Paris, where most of the important painting of
the first forty years of this century was done. He stayed a year
"painting and wandering about the streets," and found that it
reminded him of Philadelphia. "Paris was old fashioned, but
modern as well. That was the wonderful part of it . . . There was
so much of the past and the immediate present brought together
on one plane that nothing seemed left to be desired.[30] In this last
remark Davis seems indirectly to be describing the streetscapes
he made there (plates 18, 19, 21–26, 28). In their literal rendition
of the architecture of the city they belong to an old tradition of
using the picturesque subject to engage the spectator's interest.
Yet he presents his scenes in terms of his now established principles, particularly in respect to the aim of maintaining the integrity
of the canvas surface, even to the extent of calling attention to it
through heavily textured paint. *Rue des Rats No. 2* (plate 26) com-
bines a stucco-like texture with the smooth-plaster effect of oil
spread on by palette-knife. And though he draws his buildings in
with a reasonable facsimile of classic perspective, the light and
dark areas neither correspond to a consistent direction of light
nor to any principle of form as made by light. Half-closing one's
eyes one can see in *Adit No. 2* (plate 19), for example, that without
the little linear demarcations of a minor sort, the picture is made
of flat planes distributed primarily for compositional rather than
representational ends. The pictures are even flatter in color than
in black and white (plates 24, 25) because Davis has adjusted
his colors in such a way as to combat the force of the directional
lines responsible for the perspectival depth. He has used strong
value contrasts where one would expect smooth transitions, and
a continuous color-plane where one would expect differentiation,

23

as one may note in *Rue Vercingetorix* (plate 18). The scribbles in the sky, almost words, add to the unreality, and keep the paint surface active just where the eye, following the conventions of a vision trained by past painting, might take off into the blue. These Paris landscapes were consumed by fashionable commercial and advertising artists in the next decade or so, and thus have lost most of their freshness for us today—an unfortunate but logical result of art which is just a little too easy from the beginning, as in the case of some of van Gogh where, once the public grasped the notion in watered-down versions, we tired of him for the time. (When the reproductions of the *Sun Flowers* have finally faded and disappeared from daily view, we shall look at him again with refreshed, though historian's, eyes, possibly to learn some things we missed.)

In the years following Davis' return from Paris in 1929, perhaps realizing that the streetscapes were really a rest from, rather than part of, his quest for an authentic *modus operandi*, he attacked the problems of painting from an experimental variety of angles. In such a picture as *Still Life with Saw* (plate 27) he has taken a hint from Miro and the Surrealists and permitted himself a striking freedom in disposition of his subject forms. And in *Interior* (plate 30) he has abstracted the scribbles and crossed-lines from the streetscapes and used them with an almost gay self-sufficiency in a composition that has only the barest hint of the older, tighter construction. Considering these pictures in the light of his work as a whole, they would seem aberrations. The core of his painting has been the structure of landscape. Yet Davis' juxtaposition of incongruities in the masterworks of the 1940's and 1950's, as well as in the handsome little landscapes of 1933–34 (*Sunrise*, plate 37), is the secret poetry in his complex of forms. By freeing himself from the thorough-going abstractionism of the *Eggbeaters* and from the literal aspects of the Paris streetscapes, he opened up one more possibility to be gradually included in the total meaning of his pictures. Through the 1930's these narrative, descriptive and

24

symbolic suggestions are relatively obvious. The late works, however, transcend any ascribable, referential meanings (though one can enjoy the game of hunting down some of his ambiguous rabbits, (see comments on *Visa,* plate 55). Thus the words in *Package Deal* (plate 73), for example, *mean* what they say, but what they say is pictorial rather than intellectual. Words, as introduced by Davis, are to be read as visual forms, just as are the numbers and the sign for infinity and the crosses etc., and this is what he is telling you. He could not tell you in any other way except by this demonstration. If you are stopped by your inability to transcend their connotations, then you will never be able to know or appreciate words as a visual artist does, as *things* rather than as signs for abstract ideas. One may very well read the nude in the classical picture as a sign for sex, it is difficult not to, yet hardly anyone would believe that this meaning was primary in the artist's purpose. In the modern environment words and signs are continuously present to our vision. We may or may not read them as we take them into our visual experience, but they are there, red, yellow, green, big and little, unavoidable, and now even subliminal.

> *There are an infinite number of form concepts available.*[31]

Though Davis considers the question of whether a picture has depth or is flat quite irrelevant, it is manifest in his work that his taste, if nothing else, forces him to resolve such formal oppositions. During the 1930's he composed several pictures with dual views. They are like unbalanced stereopticon photographs, divided down the center—an intriguing but dangerous experiment. Surprisingly many of them succeeded, a result attributable only to the excellence of his adjusting eye. They are reminiscent

25

of *The Compote* and *The Mirror* by Léger (1925). In *House and Street* (plate 36) the images are separate and only related by similarity of treatment and projection on a common background. The effect is as if one had a view around the corner. In a group of landscapes, like the above-mentioned *Sunrise,* the two halves are fused and drawn together into an intricate web of planes defined by their linear directions. He has used this real and suggested division of the picture in recent years, too (*Lesson 1* and *Pochade,* plates 74, 75).

During the 1930's he also evolved a type of ink drawing which excellently demonstrates how many of his pictures are planned (plates 15, 19) and, indeed, how the fusions of views, planes, lines and signal forms are arrived at initially. In these it is possible to imagine the interstices filled with flat colors, continuously and carefully adjusted for both variety and cohesion, taking care not to rupture the surface tension of the canvas.

In the late 1930's and early 1940's, however, Davis must have decided that another kind of picture was susceptible to the personal style now completely at his command. It may be that the Federal Art Project commissions for murals directed his attention to the possibility of what is nowadays called "all-over" painting (mistakenly thought by some to be an invention of the Abstract-Expressionists).[32] Two murals from this period, one in Studio B of radio station WNYC in New York and *Men without Women* in Radio City Music Hall, tend toward a loose dispersal of their subject matter. While he has made an adequate solution of these particular mural problems, Davis seems to have considered that there was a better way to preserve the integrity of the wall, ultimately so essential to a mural art compatible with architecture. Modern painting is, in fact, ideally oriented toward considering such questions since it has sought so unceasingly for ways and means to preserve the reality of the surface.

Because Davis had liberated himself from subservience to Renaissance perspective in the early stages of his career, his picture tended to fill toward the edges with formal material,

26

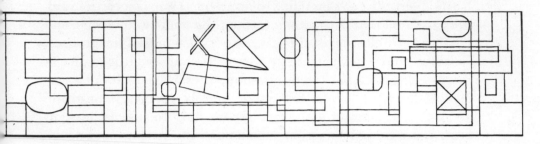

ale Drawing for Allée. 1954. 24 x 34⅛″. The Downtown Gallery

distroying focus, as I noted in the remarks on *Landscape*
In the intervening years, concerned with other problems, he
worked primarily with either large discrete forms, openly placed,
or toward a vignette surrounded by a flatly felt surface, purposely
designed to define and limit the field of space. In the mural for
the World's Fair, 1939, now destroyed, and the one at Indiana
University, *Swing Landscape* (plate 44), realizing that the
vignette would create a picture *on the wall* rather than a *wall-
picture,* and apparently dissatisfied with the way his other
method tended to chop up the wall, he flooded the wall-space to
the brim with his web of forms. In this way he was able to
achieve an evenly distributed rhythm quite concordant with the

27

truth about the eye's inability to apprehend huge pictures in any proximal relation. At the same time, the wide-angle focus, and the careful limitation of the inward-outward pull of linear direction and color contrasts, kept the wall a true wall. A glance at the drawing for *Allee* (page 27) shows how Davis laid out a surface about 8 x 32' for a four-color, purely geometric mural in 1954. A minimum of diagonals appear here to suggest a slight inner-outer movement, enough to assure vitality but not enough to puncture the wall surface.

Cubism, in both its analytical and synthetic varieties, as well as School of Paris painting in general, had retained the centralized, vignette character of pictorial organization. Dispersal of the compositional elements across the whole surface of the canvas may have been a greater traumatic break with traditional notions of the picture than almost any of the innovations of the period. Davis has never settled for one method or the other, but has created paintings since the 1938 *Swing Landscape* in both the centralized and dispersed manner. In *Report from Rockport* (plate 45) there is a sense that he has wavered between the two. In *Aboretum by Flashbulb* and *Ultramarine* (plates 49, 50) he has carried the "all-over" painting to its ultimate possibilities, and thus confirmed another addition to the modern view of art —the picture can be an autonomous, self-sustaining and *space-occupying thing.*

> *The act of painting is not a duplication of experience, but the extension of experience on the plane of formal invention.*[33]

It has often been said of American artists, particularly of our writers, that they do not live up to their youthful promise. This could never be said of Davis. He not only has had the staying-power but also the ingenuous quality of single-mindedness in an age when styles are apt to change with every new mistress. His pursuit of authenticity would seem, perhaps, to have taken longer than most, though he has produced some fine pictures at each stage along the way. Yet the pursuit found its object.

Two pictures from 1940–41, *Summer Landscape No. 2* and *New York under Gaslight* (plates 46, 47) illuminate both the manner and means by which he arrived at the pictures he wanted to paint. *Summer Landscape No. 2* is an anniversary work, painted just ten years after *Summer Landscape* (plate 31), and it translates the earlier vision into the later. While the first *Landscape* was a distillation of an observed one, the second is a distilled record of all that has gone between. The first finds formal symbols for what was seen; the second refers primarily to its constructive means. *New York Under Gaslight,* on the contrary, is a jumble of references. It is Davis creating a historical souvenir. It is a joke (note the sign and the pointing finger in lower right), not a very good one, and represents his parting shot at all of the things he was discarding from his style. And in this sense it is a confirmation of his new direction. *Summer Landscape No. 2,* one of the last pictures to contain readily recognizable elements, also confirms the new and ends the old. It points the way to the world of painting to follow where the "color-shape," in a steady stream of personal symbols, will form the objective content of each picpicture.

From 1945 on Davis paints few symbols referring to things of *this-world*. Except perhaps to Davis they are, indeed, not symbols at all, but the bald and pure means to activate and inhabit the *pictorial world* of their own making. Long ago the Cubists had chosen their still-life objects from the most banal in daily view in order to break the chain of references from the pictorial to the real world. Davis has gone farther. His "color-shapes" are his own conventional objects, personally arrived at by a process of reduction from the nature he began with (note again the changes in this respect between the two *Summer*

29

Landscapes). Though many painters since the Constructivists[34] have used abstract geometrical forms, none have developed a vocabulary capable of stating all the basic elements so completely and succinctly, each one capable of carrying its own ambiguity.

Except for an occasional use of real texture as produced by impasto, Davis has consistently used paint in the classic manner as a *medium*. It is not paint, but *color* he uses. Yet to eliminate texture from his pictures would have ruled out a valuable interacting means. Thus texture is created symbolically (and, I think, optically) by spates of dots, dashes and scribbles. These elements, however, can also double for rhythmical passages, for indications of direction and depth, and thus their ambiguities, when multiplied across the canvas in mutual relations, present the spectator with a sensuously mysterious world. Those who are sensitive to both *this-world* and the pictorial world will find there a similarity of structure, an analogous relation, which is the essence of all true art. In such formal invention we many find *the extension of experience* Davis has sought from his beginning.

The real order of art is not an ideal order, or a system of beauty, because an ideal order would be timeless, and art exists in time.[35]

When Davis set out to be a "modern artist" and to find out how to "paint the pictures" he "wanted to paint," he was seeking an *order,* not necessarily absolute and for all time, but one that might serve him as he went along. That he found one and is still adding to it becomes apparent as one reviews his pictures of the last two decades. His constancy in the search, and his equanimity in the face of all the distractions that fast moving changes of style in the art world can generate is not only amazing but heroic. The best artists rarely run in packs, where there is often more cheer but less light. The artist's purpose, as he has said, "is to live in giving importance to certain qualities in himself, which everyone presumably possesses, but which relatively few cultivate."[36]

The Notes to the Text begin on page 113.

Portrait of a Man. 1911. Watercolor, 14¾ x 10¾". Lane Collection

3. *Landscape.* Ca. 1916. Oil, 26 x 25″. Collection Mr. and Mrs. Tony Randall

4. *Multiple Views*. 1918. Oil, 47 x 35″. The Downtown Gallery

5. *Yellow Hills*. 1919. Oil, 23⅜ x 29¼". The Downtown Gallery

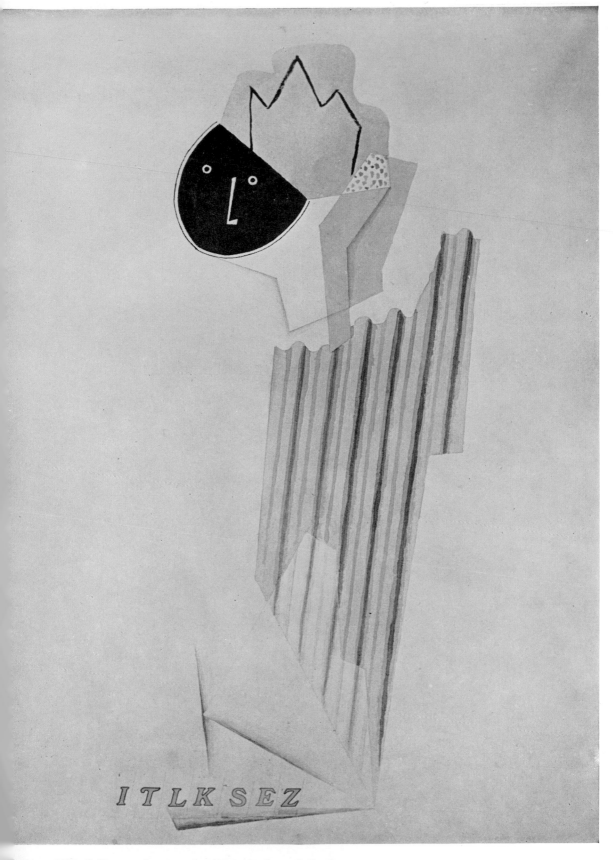

tlksez. 1921. Collage and watercolor, 22 x 16". Lane Collection

8. *Cigarette Papers*. 1921. Watercolor on canvas, 19 x 14″. Private Collection

Apples and Jug. 1923. Oil, 22 x 18″. Lane Collection

11. *Pajarito.* 1923. Oil, 22 x 36″. The Downtown Gallery

13. *Myopic Vista*. 1925. Gouache, 15 x 17". Lane Collection

14. *Super Table*. 1925. Oil, 48½ x 34⅛". The Downtown Gallery

15. *Eggbeater No. 1.* 1927. Oil, 29⅛ x 36″. Whitney Museum of American Art

16. *Eggbeater No. 3.* 1928. Oil, 25 x 39". Lane Collection

Rockport Beach. 1916. Oil, 30 x 24″. The Downtown Gallery

18. *Rue Vercingetorix.* 1928. Oil, 18 x 14¾". Collection Mr. and Mrs. John J. Carney

Adit No. 2. 1928. Oil, 29 x 24". Lane Collection

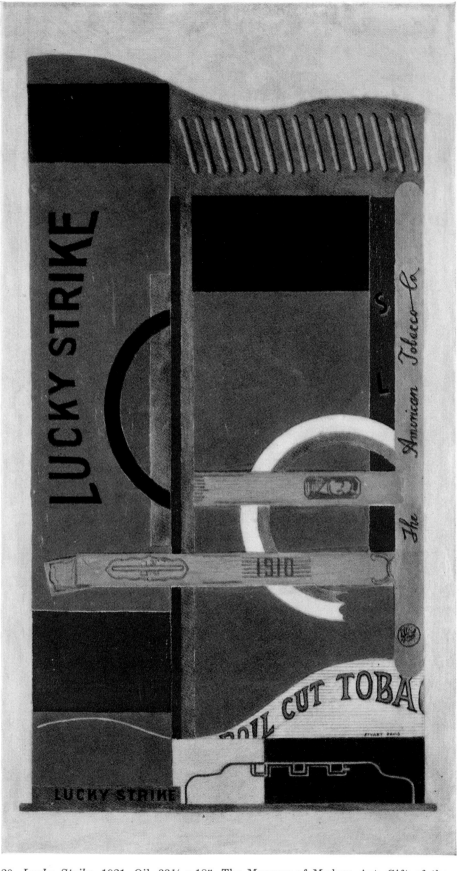

20. *Lucky Strike*. 1921. Oil, 33¼ x 18″. The Museum of Modern Art, Gift of the American Tobacco Company

21. *Place des Vosges No. 1.* 1928. Oil, 21 x 28¾". The Newark Museum

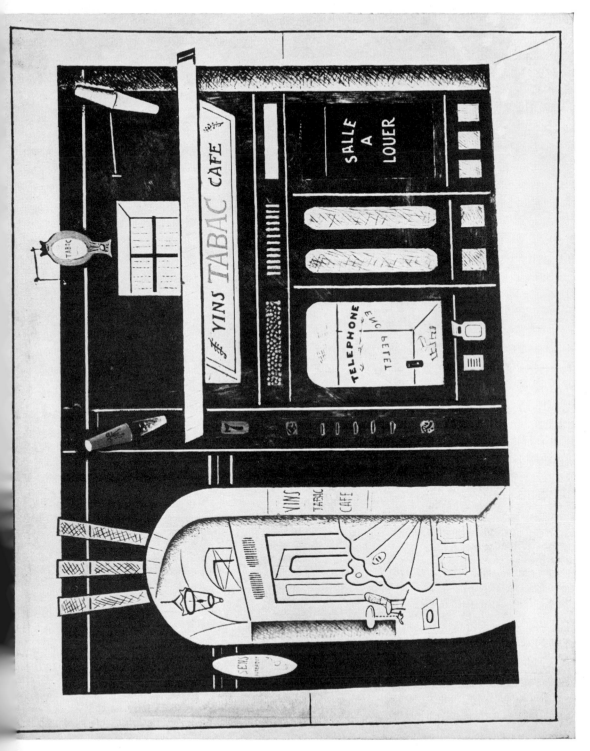

23. *Cafe, Place des Vosges.* 1929. Oil, 29 x 36¼". Collection Mrs. Edith Gregor Halpert

24. *Place Pasdeloup*. 1928

ON HIS TRIP to France in 1928–29, Davis was overpowered by scenic Paris. His abstract Eggbeater series had not fully purged him of the desire to paint directly from nature. He was not so overpowered, however, as to want to photograph it in paint or to succumb to the unguent romanticism so common to Parisian landscapes by enamoured artists. The scenes before him are excuses for making paintings, and though he has never abandoned nature and its structural relationships (Clement Greenberg has said that those paint-ers who do, "walk in the void")* Davis' development has been constantly toward essences rather than repre-sentation of the palpable world.

Here the painting reproduced in color appears flatter and less naturalistic than the one in black and white. This is because the direction of so many of the lines coincide with classical representation of linear perspective. But Davis uses relatively brilliant colors in flat planes to get rid of the atmospheric effects common to naturalistic landscape. And by alternating white and color in the rear building, where we expect a dimin-ishing of hue as effected by distance, he pulls it forward. This result is also apparent in the contrast be-tween the two reproductions at the bottom of the rear building where the wall is penetrated by an alley. In the reproduction above we feel we could walk into it; in the picture opposite, he has shut it off by identify-ing the alley with the whole facade, bringing them into one plane.

The one place where the flatness he is after fails is in the sky, where the atmospheric blue, in con-junction with the receding diagonal of the roof on the right, produces the effect of infinite airy space. He has tried to correct this with the calligraphic scribble overlaying the sky area. It is only a partial solution; our associations with blue are too strong and our eye is led out into space despite the unreasonableness of the scribble.

Davis did not invent the methods he is using here but it is interesting to see how he moves, as if he were checking the history of recent art. One feels that he has never really been anxious about being first or making world shaking *discoveries* (which so often prove to have pedigrees as long as that of the art of painting). Davis' discoveries have been for his own use, applicable to the consummation of his personal style. Apollinaire called Braque the *verifier* of Cubism. Davis has been his own verifier throughout his career.

*In "The Role of Nature in Modern Art," *Partisan Review*, Jan. 1949, pp. 78–81

Place Pasdeloup. 1928. Oil, 36⅛ x 28½". Whitney Museum of American Art

27. *Still Life With Saw.* 1930. Oil, 26 x 34″. The Phillips Collection, Washington

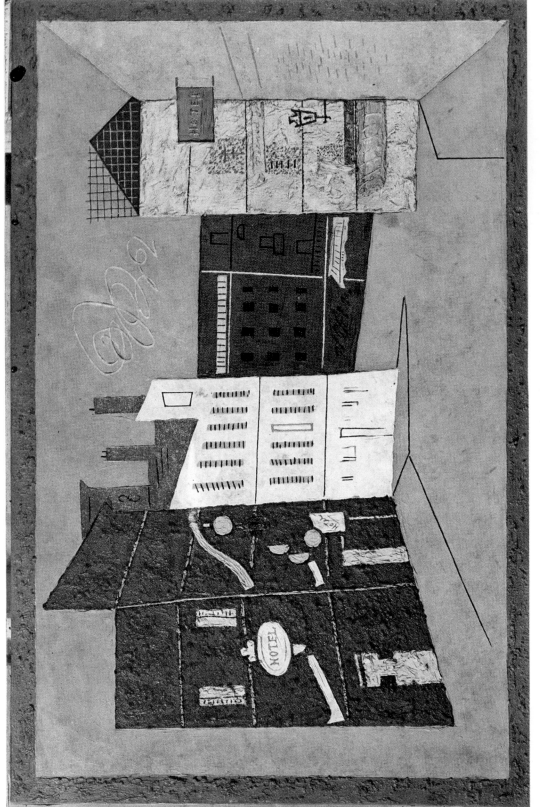

28. *Rue de l'Echaude.* 1929. Oil, 23⅝ x 38¾". Collection Mr. Otto L. Spaeth

29. *Eggbeater No. 5*. 1930. Oil, 50⅛ x 32¼". The Museum of Modern Art,
Mrs. John D. Rockefeller, Jr. Fund

30. *Interior*. 1930. Oil, 24 x 20″. Collection Mr. George Hopper Fitch

31. *Summer Landscape.* 1930. Oil, 29 x 42". The Museum of Modern Art, Purchase

Salt Shaker is a brilliant, off-beat picture painted during one of Davis' most prolific periods, just after his return from Paris and just before the necessarily decreased output of the Depression years. Though it is of that variety of late Cubism which tended toward Surrealism (Picasso's *Three Musicians*, for example) it is entirely Davis' own picture. The Surrealist element is contained wholly in the suggestion of a ghostly mask in the top of the salt shaker turned flat against the canvas. The Cubist element is, of course, in the metamorphosis of the round object into an extended flat one. Davis' skill in tying the shaker to the rectangle of the canvas is evident in the three red slashes acting like cleats, with their accompanying spot to place them exactly. Following Cubist practice in presenting at least one form as projecting outward, or having at minimum the illusion of volume, the narrow piece coming down from the corner is given a cast shadow and a twist at the end. This object also serves to bind the shaker, which would otherwise be indeterminately loose in its field of stripes, to the edge of the rectangle. It holds it in lateral position and eliminates the possibility of a vignette effect. The rhomboidal bottom also adds spatial depth, aided by the curious arrow.

Unless I am mistaken, the striped background is Davis' own invention. It identifies the surface of the canvas in an odd way, making it breathe, as it were, and providing a dominant textural differentiation against which the plain surfaces, the grids, and the brushed and dotted areas can act all the more vitally.

32. *Salt Shaker*. 1931. Oil, 49⅞ x 32". The Museum of Modern Art,
Gift of Mrs. Edith Gregor Halpert

33. ABOVE: *New York—Paris No. 1.* 1931. Oil, 38¼ x 51″. University of Iowa
34. BELOW: *New York—Paris No. 3.* 1931. 39 x 52″. Collection Dr. Michael W. Watter

35. *Summer Twilight*. 1931. Oil, 36 x 24″. Collection Mr. and Mrs. Lawrence Fleischman

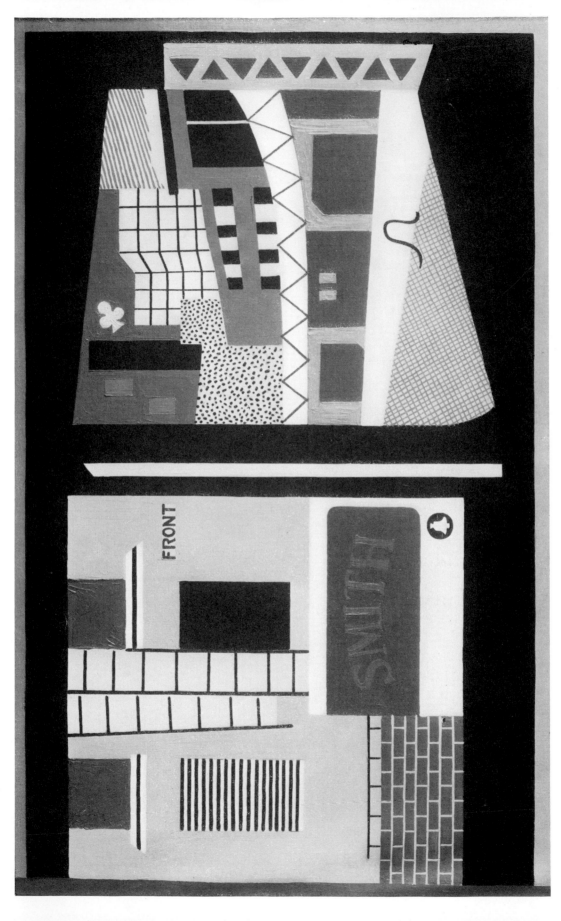

37. *Sunrise*. 1933. Oil, 10 x 14". Collection Mr. and Mrs. Holger Cahill

38. *Television.* 1932. Gouache, 10½ x 18". Collection Mr. and Mrs. Lawrence Fleischman

39. *Cigarette Papers.* 1933. Oil, 12 x 12⅜". Collection Mr. and Mrs. Holger Cahill

41. *Bass Rocks No. 1.* 1939. Oil, 43 x 33". Roland P. Murdock Collection, Wichita Art Museum

43. *Swing Landscape*. 1938. Oil, 7 x 14'. Collection Indiana University

DAVIS ONCE said that "the title of my painting is reasonable in the same way as the image itself."* Though he was referring to another picture, we can assume it applies to most of his late paintings, if not to all. If we look at *Hot Stillscape in Six Colors* with this in mind it may help to understand how Davis himself views his picture.

The picture is "hot" because Davis, using the classic language of warm and cool colors, is taking note of the fact that besides the three primary colors, red, yellow and blue, plus black and white, he has added only one secondary, orange, a combination of red and yellow. Thus the picture is geared toward the warm colors, toward the hotness of red. Had he also used green and violet he would have neutralized the color scheme, assuming, of course, that they were adjusted in more or less even proportions (not necessarily exact in *area*). Furthermore, by saying "six colors" Davis has implied that he uses black and white definitely as colors, and we can see that here they certainly do act as such. The light blue serves to key for us the precise degree of hotness and permits the picture to be its own judge.

One can see in this picture how Davis, by use of color, destroys or inhibits potential perspectival movements inward along the diagonals and tapered forms. Warm colors are classically said to come forward, while colors in the blue, green and violet range tend to recede. While Davis is not systematic in any mechanical sense, his colors are carefully plotted to keep the eye playing over the surface. There are no deep holes in this picture. And though there is a slight suggestion of room for his "color shapes" to breathe, the absence of any directed light *within* the picture prevents shadows forming and thus intimating that the shapes have volume. The five circles at the lower right suggest balls on the one hand, but their volumetric existence is put in question by the fact that the side from which light *might* have come is different in each case. There is no reference to a light source as we observe it in naturalistic painting and in the world of light and shade around us.

The word "stillscape" in the title also implies that he thinks of this painting as a combination of *still-life* and *landscape*. If one looks at it closely some of the forms begin to appear as things we could recognize, but not to the same degree as in earlier works, or even as in his *Report from Rockport* of the same year. As time goes on, Davis stretches the analogy between his shapes and objects in nature even farther.

*From a statement in *Contemporary American Painting* (an exhibition catalogue), Urbana, University of Illinois, 1952, p. 183–4

44. *Hot Stillscape for Six Colors.* 1940. Oil, 36 x 45". Collection Mrs. Edith Gregor Halpert

Stuart Davis. *Report from Rockport.* 1940. Oil. 24 x 30". Collection Edith and Milton Lowenthal

46. *Summer Landscape No. 2.* 1940. Oil, 8 x 12". Collection Mr. Charles Alan

48. *Ursine Park.* 1942. Oil, 20 x 40". Collection IBM Corp.

49. *Arboretum by Flashbulb.* 1942. Oil, 18 x 36″. Collection Edith and Milton Lowenthal

50. *Ultramarine.* 1943. Oil, 20 x 40″. The Pennsylvania Academy of the Fine Arts

51. *The Mellow Pad.* 1945-51. Oil, 26 x42″. Collection Edith and Milton Lowenthal

52. *For Internal Use Only*. 1945. Oil, 45 x 28". Collection Mr. and Mrs. Burton G. Tremaine, Jr.

Stuart Davis

54. *Max No. 2.* 1949. Oil, 12 x 16″. Washington University

PROBABLY BECAUSE Davis had been encouraged by Henri back in 1910 to wander the streets and draw the life around him, he developed an astute eye for whatever might be useful to his art. One day a package of book matches advertising a famous brand of spark-plugs fell into his hand. Stimulated by the clever design, and undoubtedly the legend, he turned it to account and painted his *Little Giant Still Life* (page 11). *Visa* is the second version of that work, painted the following year.

Davis dislikes having his pictures *read* as symbolic literature, a perfectly legitimate attitude, though people are bound to do so, especially because of his frequent use of letters and words. But, as noted in the foregoing text, Davis' words and letters are there *primarily* as familiar visual *forms* in our environment and as such requisitionable material for the painter. Nevertheless the temptation in the case of *Visa* is too great. It fits the subject of this book too well.

One might pursue such a line as this: The essence of a "champion" lies in his "amazing continuity." Either he has it or "else." And it is this amazing continuity which is his "visa" to the world. The bearer may proceed. *Visa* also comes from the Latin, *videre*, to see, the artist's business after all.

Knowing Davis' admiration for professionals, whether they be painters or top jazz men like Earl Hines and George Wetling, or the best in the field of sports (an admiration he shares with Ernest Hemingway, another professional), the content of the word "Champion" grows autobiographical. One is struck by the amazing continuity of Davis' own work through the years, which divides less into periods and violent switches of style, the fits and starts one is apt to find among the more "romantic" painters. Davis' cool approach has paid off in this respect. His work has changed and changed again, yet the inimitable personal tradition, evolving rather than erupting, has given him the same sort of surprising permanence as a champion—one recalls Babe Ruth and Joe Louis. He is somebody who can do it, and do it again. If he repeats himself, it is in a new way; if he changes, he retains something of the old. He values the professional, prefers to be a professional, and so has tapped, in a jointless time, the classical element in Western civilization, the quality that produced Greek sculpture and Roman lawyers.

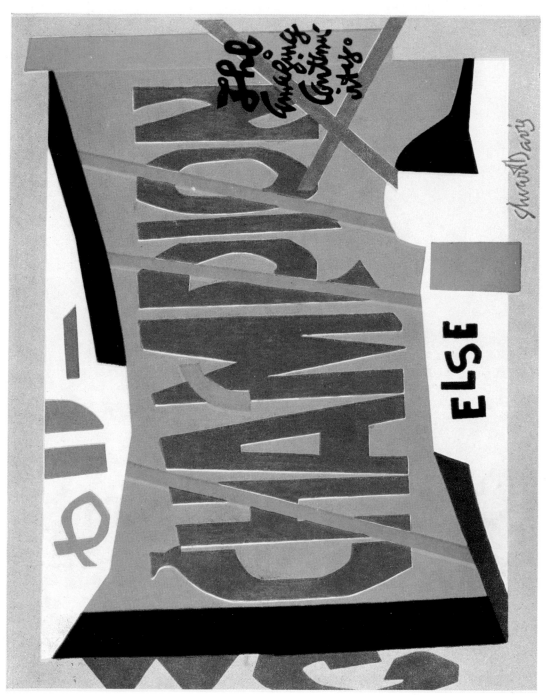

55. *Visa.* 1951. Oil, 40 x 52". The Museum of Modern Art, Gift of Mrs. Gertrud A. Mellon

7. *Rapt at Rappaport's*. 1952. Oil, 52 x 40″. Collection Mr. Joseph H. Hirshhorn

58. *Nu.* 1953. Oil, 8 x 6". Collection Mr. Ira Herbert

Medium Still Life. 1953. Oil, 44 x 36". Collection Mr. and Mrs. Daniel Saidenberg

60. *Seme*. 1953. Oil, 52 x 40″. The Metropolitan Museum of Art

1. *Eye Level.* 1954. Oil, 17 x 12". Lane Collection

62. *Shapes of Landscape Space.* 1939. Oil, 36 x 28″. Collection
Mr. Roy Neuberger

DAVIS HAS frequently returned to the compositions of his earlier pictures, translating
them into a later manner. The *Tournos* image is derived from "Shapes of Landscape
Space" and an even earlier drawing executed in 1932. It is not that he is haunted by a
particular subject, but proves quite the opposite, that subject-matter is merely an
impetus, a spark-plug for an esthetic end. The *esthetic* qualities in the older pictures
stimulate him to carry them forward. In each subsequent version he has advanced the
picture toward the purified constructional principles of his evolving "color-space" ideas.
By revising his works to bring them nearer the ones he "want(ed) to paint" (which
perhaps recede like Gatsby's green light), he is recognizing the values of both permanence and change. His esthetic, he seems to be saying, is amenable to its own revela-
tions, bridging the gap between Being and Becoming, between the absolute and the
transient. And indirectly he is making a comment on the history of art (and civilization), pointing out that we are doing the same old things in new ways. For Davis, of
course, it is an assist to continuity, a way of correcting himself without jettisoning *all*
of his former values and views. It is a conservative attitude which nevertheless wisely
permits progress and the *vital* demands of time and mutation.

Tournos. 1954. Oil, 35⅞ x 28". Munson-Williams-Proctor Institute

64. *Deuce*. 1954. Oil, 26 x 42". San Francisco Museum of Art

65. *Midi.* 1954. Oil, 28 x 36". Wadsworth Atheneum, Hartford

IN RECENT years Davis has manipulated flat sharp silhouetted color-shapes in a manner related to Cubist collages. In the latter, pieces of paper were torn or cut and pasted to the canvas to achieve a pleasing or provocative arrangement, usually including drawing, and striving toward a heightening of the esthetic powers of the real materials of everyday life. The essential quality of Cubist work in general was *ambiguity*, an ambiguity born in the marriage of self-evident realities with self-evident illusions. Cubist color, however, even at its most intense, never approached anything like Davis' brilliant hues. Some people feel his color is garish, while others see it as a comment on the sensational competition to which we submit ourselves everyday without being particularly aware of it. Van Gogh's color was criticized as garish at its first appearance.

While he says that he has no color *formula*, that he begins arbitrarily, one can see how, in *Colonial Cubism*, Davis carefully establishes his four blue shapes in three separate planes, and his reds, blacks, oranges and whites on at least two. The result is a kind of Chinese puzzle. Tension is created through the ambiguous relation between the parts and their position in a thin space, and also by such interventions as the black rhomboid on white (top center) which destroys the continuity of the black horizontal figure beneath it. Colors disappearing beneath other color planes emerge unexpectedly altered on the other side, often changing color or changing planes in the process. Every graphic means toward tension and ambiguity is exploited.

The crisp clarity of Davis' shapes and his pristine color are reminiscent of Fernand Léger, whom he admired and who developed early and speedily among the Cubists (Picasso, Braque, Metzinger, Gleizes and Gris). Léger, however, nearly always used rounded forms in combination with flat ones. Davis' paintings are more austere in their flatness but more brilliant in color, even though Léger also employed a bright, limited palette. Unlike Léger, who introduced the human figure drawn as if it were a machine, Davis has almost entirely avoided it. He feels that whatever man makes is intrinsically, and therefore sufficiently, human in character.

66. *Colonial Cubism*. 1954. Oil, 45 x 60". Walker Art Center

67. *Ready to Wear*. 1955. Oil, 56 x 42″. The Art Institute of Chicago

Cliché. 1955. Oil, 56 x 42". The Solomon R. Guggenheim Museum

Something on the Eight Ball. 1954. Oil, 56 x 45″. Philadelphia Museum of Art

71. *Study for Mural—U.N. Conference Room 3.* 1956. Oil, 28 x 70". Lane Collection

72. *Lesson I.* 1956. Oil, 42 x 60". The Downtown Gallery

73. *Package Deal.* 1956. Gouache, 20¾ x 18″. The Downtown Gallery

Bridge at Courbevoie. 1956. Oil, 10½ x 8″. Collection Mr. and Mrs. Allan D. Emil

6. *Famous Firsts*. 1958. Oil, 36 x 27″. In the Brooklyn Museum Collection,
Dick S. Ramsey and J. B. Woodward Funds

77. *Combination Concrete*. 1958. Oil, 71 x 53". Collection Mr. and Mrs. Earl Wade Hubbard

NOTES TO THE TEXT

1. Davis, Stuart, *Stuart Davis,* no pagination, (American Artists Group, New York, 1945).
2. *Commitment* is a word popular among artists one or two generations younger than Davis. It is derived from the *engagement* of the French Existentialists meaning, rather loosely, to devote oneself *utterly* to something such as painting or politics even though everything is absurd.
3. Edward W. Davis. Stuart's mother was a sculptress, Helen Stuart Foulke.
4. A short, lively account of "The Eight" and their times can be found in *Arts Yearbook 1,* p. 57 ff, by Leslie Katz. N.Y. 1957.
5. Robert Henri was not a Philadelphian by birth nor was his last name Henri, implying French ancestry. His father was a gambler named Cozad who roamed the Far West. Henri's middle name was Henry, which he converted when he dropped Cozad forever.
6. Davis, *op. cit.*
7. Hans Hofmann's schools on Eighth Street in New York and in Provincetown have been perhaps the greatest single influence on American postwar painting. Hofmann came to this country from Munich, where he also had had a school, in the early '30s. Though he has retired from teaching, he is, in his seventies, one of the best known and highly respected painters identified with Abstract-Expressionism.
8. Davis, *op. cit.*
9. *Ibid.*

113

10. *Ibid.*
11. *Ibid.*
12. "a radical magazine," Davis in *Stuart Davis, op. cit.*
13. Davis writes in his biography, op. cit. from 1933 "until 1939, through the W.P.A. Art Project, with its paupers' oath, I painted for the Federal and Municipal governments. Two murals were included in the process. This accounts for the scarcity of available or privately owned works by myself during the period. Another contributing factor was the prevalence of meetings, petitions, picket lines, arrests, Artists' Unions and the Artists' Congress, in all of which I enthusiastically participated. At one point I was editor of *Art Front,* a lively Artists' Union magazine."
14. Accounts of the Armory Show, as it is now usually called, are included in all recent histories of American art. Though the new European art had been shown in small galleries around New York for several years the scale of its revolutionary character was not widely known or understood by many artists as well as the public at large.
15. Davis, *op. cit.*
16. Wild Beasts; so called because of their radical use of color contrary to naturalistic representation and academic "laws."
17. Demuth was an American from Lancaster, Pa., who had traveled abroad and knew what was going on first hand. He adapted certain of the geometrical suggestions of Cubism to his landscapes. Also known for his charming watercolors and his illustrations of Henry James' stories.
18. Marsden Hartley, painter and poet, best known for his expressionistic landscapes of the Maine coast. Arshile Gorky, an Armenian-American, painted thickly and rawly in the '30s, but later changed to a thinly delicate style, Surrealist, but with a manner which had wide effect on postwar Expressionists.
19. Davis, *op. cit.*
20. "Art in Painting," *Marsden Hartley and Stuart Davis* (exhibition catalogue), Cincinnati. Cincinnati Modern Art Society, 1941.
21. Davis is not guilty. Like Léger's, his mural work has always taken the architecture into account and he did not paint murals until he had a style quite opposite to the kind referred to here.
22. Sweeney, James Johnson, *Stuart Davis* (New York, Museum of Modern Art, 1945), p. 16.
23. Japanese artist, 1760–1849, one of those whom Davis has cited as an influence.

24. Sweeney, James Johnson, *op. cit.* p. 17.
25. *Ibid.* p. 16.
26. *Ibid.* p. 17.
27. *Ibid.* pp. 16–17.
28. "Is There a Revolution in the Arts?" *Bulletin of America's Town Meeting of the Air,* v. 5, no. 19 (Feb. 19, 1940), p. 13.
29. Sweeney, James Johnson, *op. cit.* p. 20.
30. *Ibid.* p. 19.
31. Downtown Gallery catalogue to Davis show, New York, March 1931.
32. Abstract-Expressionist is the general, very loose and largely misused name for postwar New York artists.
33. "What About Modern Art and Democracy?" *Harper's Magazine,* v. 188 (Dec. 1943), p. 34.
34. The Constructivists were a group of artists originally associated with the Suprematists in Russia (1913). They left the country for Germany in 1920, and, as the name implies, they felt that in an age of machines and industry the materials of art should be modern; steel, wire, chromium, etc., and the method *construction* rather than painting. Most notable of the group still alive are the brothers, Naum Gabo and Antoine Pevsner.
35. "Is There a Revolution in the Arts?", *op. cit.* p. 13.
36. Sweeney, James Johnson, *op. cit.* p. 5.

COMMENTS AND ADDENDA

IN THE FOREGOING analytical narrative of Stuart Davis' development I have left out a number of things other writers might have included. One of them is Davis' interest in American jazz. While I recognize the possible analogies one may draw from this interest, an article by John Lucas (see bibliography) seems to have more than covered the point. The number of artists, American and foreign, who like jazz would come to about 90 per cent of the total. I am aware, nevertheless, that Davis was one of the earliest to seek it out and appreciate it, and perhaps to discover some esthetic ideas in it for his art. But to me the most important thing about Davis' work, and Davis, for that matter, is the fact that he worked so long and so carefully building his esthetic principles in order to create some great pictures by means of them. I seem to see him as an arc with one end embedded in the kind of concrete Cubism was made of and the other end projecting somewhere into the near future when the demand for equally concrete and governing principles may assist the *younger,* younger generation (the next?) in finding themselves with less pain than has been possible recently. The dynamics of Form and Freedom will probably continue, however.

I am also doubtful if the heavy emphasis usually put on the Americanness of Davis' subject matter is any longer a moot point. Davis' use of the local scene, his gas pumps, gas stations, billboards, etc., have occupied many columns of print. I might note that in the few years since his one-man show at the International Exhibition, the Biennale in Venice, *Supermaggiore* gas stations have mushroomed all over Italy, to the extent that traveling along, ignoring an occasional medieval tower on the horizon, one could be driving almost anywhere in the American countryside. What is peculiarly American, it would seem, may be vanishing from the world.

117

CHRONOLOGY

1894   Born Philadelphia, December 7.

1901   To East Orange, New Jersey.

1910   Left high school to study with Robert Henri. Exhibited with the Independents.

1913   Did covers and drawings for *The Masses*. Exhibited five watercolors in the International Exhibition of Modern Art (known as the Armory Show). Cartoons for *Harper's Weekly;* summer, Provincetown.

1915   First summer at Gloucester.

1917   First one-man show at Sheridan Square Gallery, New York.

1918   Made maps for Army Intelligence. Trip to Havana to recover from flu with friend, Glenn O. Coleman.

1923   To New Mexico for summer.

1925   One-man show at Newark Museum.

1927   First one-man show with Downtown Gallery (Edith Gregor Halpert, his dealer). Has shown with Downtown since.

1928   *Eggbeater* series. To Paris in spring.

1929   Return to New York from Paris, late summer; to Gloucester.

1931   Began teaching at Art Students League.

1932   Mural for Radio City Music Hall.

1933   Joined Federal Art Project.

1934–39 Associated with Artists' Congress, editor, *Art Front,* executed W.P.A. murals and one for Hall of Communication at New York World's Fair.

1940   Resigned Artists' Congress. Began teaching at The New School for Social Research, New York.

1941   Retrospective exhibitions at Indiana University and Cincinnati Modern Art Society.
1945   Retrospective at Museum of Modern Art.
1956   Shown at the XXVIIIrd Biennale in Venice.
1957   Retrospective exhibition organized by Walker Art Center, Minneapolis, in collaboration with Des Moines Art Center, San Francisco Museum of Art, and the Whitney Museum of American Art, New York.

SELECTED BIBLIOGRAPHY

THIS BIBLIOGRAPHY is not intended to be complete. Most newspaper reviews have not been included and only those magazine reviews have been entered which the author deems important enough to assist the discriminating general reader. Davis has had wide attention in the press throughout his career, but much of it, from the point of view of pertinence, is repetitive, inconsequential or normally unavailable. All titles are listed chronologically.

Statements and Writings by Davis

"Self Interview," *Creative Art,* v. 9. Sept., 1931, p. 208–11.
"The Artist Today: The Standpoint of the Artists' Union," *American Magazine of Art,* v. 28, Aug., 1935, pp. 476–78, 506.
"The American Artists' Congress," *Art Front,* v. 2, no. 8, Dec., 1935, p. 8.
"Art and the Masses," *Art Digest,* v. 14, Oct. 1, 1939, pp. 13, 34.
"Davis Explains His Resignation from Artists' Congress," *New York Times,* April 14, 1940, sec. 9, p. 9.
"Stuart Davis," *Parnassus,* v. 12, no. 8, Dec., 1940, p. 6.
"Abstract Art in the American Scene," *Parnassus,* v. 13, March, 1941, pp. 100–3.
"Art in Painting," *Marsden Hartley and Stuart Davis,* Cincinnati, Cincinnati Modern Art Society, 1941, p. 7–8. Exh. Catalogue.
"The Cube Root," *Art News,* v. 41, Feb. 1, 1943, pp. 22–3, 33–4.
Stuart Davis, Stuart Davis, New York, American Artists Group, 1945, 64 pp., monograph.
"What Abstract Art Means to Me," *Museum of Modern Art Bulletin,* v. 18, no. 3, Spr. 1951, pp. 14–15.
"Symposium: The Creative Process," *Art Digest,* v. 28, Jan. 1954, pp. 16, 34.

On Davis

Paul, Eliot. "Stuart Davis, American Painter," *Transition,* no. 14, 1928, pp. 146–48.

Gorky, Arshile. "Stuart Davis," *Creative Art,* v. 9, Sept., 1931, pp. 212–17.

"Stuart Davis, the Difficult," *Art Digest,* v. 6, April 1, 1932, p. 2.

"Stuart Davis and Abstraction," *Art Digest,* v. 8, May 15, 1934, p. 14.

"Hot Still-Scapes for Six Colors—7th Ave. Style," *Parnassus,* v. 12, Dec., 1940, p. 6.

Current Biography . . . 1940, New York, H. W. Wilson, 1940, pp. 228–29.

Barr, Alfred H., Jr. *What Is Modern Painting?,* New York, Museum of Modern Art, 1943, p. 4–5.

Janis, Sidney. *Abstract and Surrealistic Art in America,* New York, Reynal & Hitchcock, 1944, pp. 50, 53.

Sweeney, James Johnson. *Stuart Davis.* New York, Museum of Modern Art, 1945.

Cahill, Holger. "In Retrospect 1945–1910," *Art News,* v. 44, Oct. 15, 1945, pp. 24–5, 32.

Coates, Robert M. "Retrospective of Paintings: Modern Museum," *New Yorker,* v. 21, Oct. 27, 1945, p. 52.

Wolf, Ben. "Stuart Davis: 30 Years of Evolution," *Art Digest,* v. 20, Nov. 1, 1945, pp. 10, 34.

Greenberg, Clement. Review of Stuart Davis Exhibition, *Nation,* v. 161, Nov. 17, 1945.

Wolf, Ben. "The Digest Interviews Stuart Davis," *Art Digest,* v. 20, Dec. 15, 1945, p. 21.

Sargeant, Winthrop. "Why Artists Are Going Abstract, The Case of Stuart Davis," *Life,* v. 22, Feb. 17, 1947, pp. 78–81, 83.

"Virginia Museum Picks its Winners in 1950 Biennial," *Art Digest,* v. 24, May 15, 1950, p. 17.

"Winner of the Seventh Biennial Exhibition at the Virginia Museum," *Art News,* v. 49, June 1950, p. 9.

Loucheim, Aline B. "Six Abstractionists Defend Their Art," *New York Times Magazine,* Jan. 21, 1951, sec. 6, pp. 16–17.

"Very Free Association; Critics Battle over Davis *Little Giant Still-Life* at the Virginia Museum of Fine Arts," *Art Digest,* v. 26, March 15, 1952, p. 5

"Paintings Sent to the Biennal in Venice Shown at Downtown Gallery," *Art News,* v. 51, Jan. 1953, p. 45.

Wight, Frederick S. "Stuart Davis," *Art Digest,* v. 27, May 15, 1953, pp. 13, 23.

Seckler, Dorothy Gees. "Stuart Davis Paints a Picture," *Art News,* v. 52, Summer, 1953, pp. 30–3, 73–4.

Coates, Robert M. "Exhibition at Downtown Gallery," *New Yorker,* v. 30, March 20, 1954, pp. 81–2.

"The Jazzy Formalism of Stuart Davis," *Art News,* v. 53, March, 1954, pp. 19, 59.

Kramer, Hilton. "Month in Review," *Arts,* v. 31, Nov. 1956, p. 52–55.

T. P. Stuart Davis. Stuart Davis, *Art News,* v. 55, Nov. 1956, p. 6.

Blesh, Rudi. *Modern Art, U.S.A.,* New York, Alfred A. Knopf, 1956, pp. 17, 48, 51, 96, 107, 127, 133, 178, 179, 183, 258.

de Kooning, Elaine. "Stuart Davis: True to Life," *Art News,* v. 56, no. 2, April 1957, pp. 41–42, 54–55.

Lucas, John. "The Fine Art Jive of Stuart Davis," *Arts,* Sept. 1957, v. 31. no. 10, pp. 32–37.

Arnason, H. H. "Stuart Davis" Catalogue Introduction, An Exhibition by the Walker Art Center, Minneapolis, in collaboration with the Des Moines Art Center, San Francisco Museum of Art, and the Whitney Museum of American Art, New York; 1958.

A., J. "Stuart Davis: Is Today's Artist With or Against the Past?" An Interview. *Art News,* Summer, 1958, v. 57, no. 4, p. 43.

PHOTOGRAPHIC CREDITS

The photographs in this book are reproduced through the courtesy of Oliver Baker except for those listed below.

Andover Art Studio   1, 7, 19
Ferdinand Boesch   37, 48
Colton of N. Y.   16, 33, 42, 45, 46, 47, 53, 62
Conde Nast Publication Inc.   28
Percy Rainford   13
Sandak, Inc.   25, 41
Soichi Sunami   2, 5, 8, 14, 27, 31, 35, 36
Mr. and Mrs. Burton G. Tremaine, Jr.   52

INDEX

The roman numerals refer to text references, the *italic* numerals to the black and white plates, and the **bold face** numerals to the color plates. The titles of the reproductions are listed in *italics*.